paper SERIES

Also by David Yee

lady in the red dress

PAPER SERIES
DAVID YEE

PLAYWRIGHTS CANADA PRESS
TORONTO

PLAYWRIGHTS CANADA PRESS
269 Richmond St. W., Suite 202, Toronto, ON M5V 1X1
416.703.0013 • info@playwrightscanada.com • www.playwrightscanada.com

We acknowledge the financial support of the Canada Council for the Arts,
the Ontario Arts Council, the Ontario Media Development Corporation, and
the Government of Canada through the Canada Book Fund for our publishing
activities.

 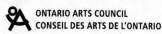

Cover art and design by Leon Aureus
Book design by Blake Sproule

LIBRARY AND ARCHIVES CANADA CATALOGUING IN PUBLICATION
Yee, David, 1977-
    Paper series / David Yee.

A play.
Issued also in electronic format.
ISBN 978-1-77091-104-8

    I. Title.

PS8647.E44P36 2012   C812'.6   C2012-904505-5

First edition: October 2012
Printed and bound in Canada by Imprimerie Gauvin, Gatineau

for liana

foreword

I knew David Yee as a person before I knew his work as a writer; each time I met him I was impressed with his sardonic sense of self, his ironically detached awareness of his place in the world and his embracing of his inner brat. *paper SERIES* was the first play of his I had seen and I approached the opening-night performance with a clear expectation of what to expect. I was so wrong. This was a production—beautifully directed by Nina Lee Aquino for Cahoots Theatre—that was neither sardonic nor ironic, though perhaps a little bratty in the best possible sense. I was delighted and disturbed in a way that the play I expected to see could have never delighted or disturbed. I suppose I expected to see a play that would be about ideas—aware and detached. I was not expecting such heart, such intelligent, exposed, unapologetic yet beseeching heart. Walking away from the production I wondered if perhaps I was seeing Nina's heart more than David's. Maybe on paper *paper SERIES* would be just that little bit colder, angrier, more damning than hopeful. Then I read the play. I was wrong again. Yes, here are the worlds of outcasts and misfits, the Mutts and criminals, the denied and the denying, the leaving and the stuck, but in these worlds we see ourselves, our mothers and fathers, our children, our lovers, our doctors and cab drivers. David presents how we judge and how we feel judged. He makes us a part. He reminds us of our heart and how in the end it's all that matters. And that is delightful. And yet there is something disturbing here—this is not a sweet floss, no up-with-people-esqueness. David understands those things that stand in the way of us accessing our hearts, those seemingly insurmountable things, the roles we have been cast in and the stories we seem to be destined to continue to tell. How we are all somehow dolls to some force outside our control, searching for a route out, to escape the burns and cuts and tears, to find a fold. We are the paper.

In his notes David says that *paper SERIES* is not a play but an anthology. At first I thought, no; this I felt was not accurate, my sense of an anthology being a thing cold and disconnected from itself, something literary, an intended device rather than a complete single thing, expressive. Certainly my response to seeing and reading the work was a feeling of connectedness, to the world, to myself and to a sense of David and his genius for showing the surface and the underneath at the same time. Wasn't this what a play was? And then I did a brief investigation into the etymology of the word and discovered that anthology comes from the Greek *anthologia* meaning "bouquet of flowers." So there I was, wrong again. *paper SERIES* is most clearly and profoundly that, a thing of delicacy and beauty. But beware, look past the bouquet into the eyes of the bearer, there is a twinkle of the brat in his eyes, and amid the blossoms there are thorns.

—Daniel MacIvor, 2012

paper SERIES was first produced at the 2007 SummerWorks Theatre Festival by the Paper Series Collective at the Factory Theatre Mainspace with the following company:

Baht: Grace Lynn Kung
Hope: Anita Majumdar
Mutt: Laura Miyata
Wisdom: David Yee
Symbol: Byron Abalos
Isaac: Ash Knight

The play was subsequently produced by Cahoots Theatre Company at the Young Centre for the Performing Arts, Toronto, between March 18 and April 9, 2011, and at the Magnetic North Theatre Festival in Calgary from June 19 to June 23, 2012. The productions featured the following cast and creative team:

Baht: Marjorie Chan
Hope: Rosa Laborde (Toronto) and Shira Leuchter (Calgary)
Mutt: Rebecca Applebaum
Wisdom: Nicco Lorenzo Garcia
Symbol: Byron Abalos
Isaac: Kawa Ada

Director: Nina Lee Aquino
Set and costume design: Camellia Koo
Lighting design: Michelle Ramsay
Sound design: Richard Lee

paper SERIES was developed with the generous support of Diaspora Dialogues, fu-GEN Asian Canadian Theatre Company and the Ontario Arts Council Theatre Creator's Reserve, as recommended by Native Earth Performing Arts. It was first presented in Factory Theatre's Performance Spring Festival and later produced at the 2007 SummerWorks Festival by the Paper Series Collective.

note

This is not a play.

This is an anthology of plays.

They are small plays, all six of them, but they are complete and written to stand alone if necessary. However, that isn't to say that they *should* be performed apart. They shouldn't. Please don't.

Although each individual piece can be performed by one actor playing all roles, in the original production the various "support-ing" roles were played by members of the ensemble. Logic and style of direction should dictate how (or if) this is done in future productions.

Just a bit about the process: *paper SERIES* represents about five years of writing. In total, I wrote somewhere in the neighbourhood of twenty-five plays... finally settling on these six. The curation of these pieces was in pursuit of an emotional arc. Each separate play, in and of itself, contains a structural narrative arc... but the trick of an anthology, I've found, is to construct something less tangible and—sometimes—greater than the sum of its parts. Although the plays stand alone, each dramaturgical change had to be weighted in context to the flow of the anthology. I don't know if that description of the process makes sense to anyone else, I don't know if it's actually valid or holds water in any other glass but my own... but in the case that it's helpful to anyone trying to create something anthological in their own work, that's what I've learned. And, like most things I've learned, it was preceded by spectacular failure and self-derision.

I guess the last thing I want to say in these notes is... thank you. Thank you for buying this book. For reading these words. If you're producing the play, thanks for putting it up. There's plenty of options out there in the big, bad world... and you chose me. I hope it's the last mistake you make all day.

—David Yee, Bali, 2012

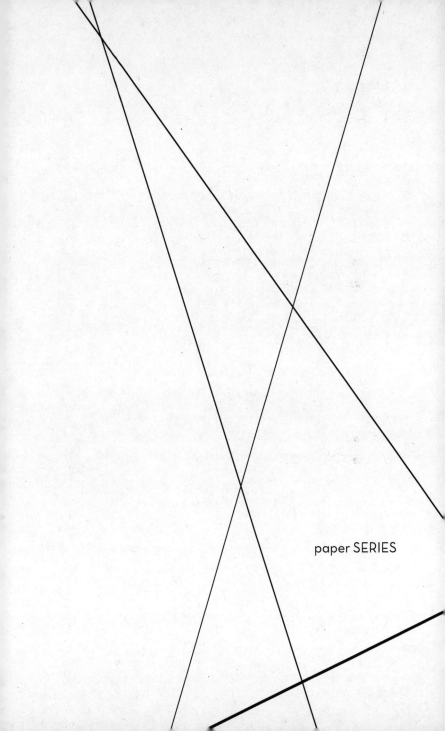

paper SERIES

characters

Baht
Hope
Mutt
Wisdom
Symbol
Isaac

PAPER burns

BAHT stands under a lit forty-watt bulb. She blows on it and watches it swing. She does this a few times, then takes a lighter out of her pocket. She takes incense sticks out of another pocket. She holds them both and examines them. Satisfied, she takes one stick of incense and lights it.

BAHT   There are six ways to get out of class when you are in elementary school. A note from your doctor. A school assembly. A physical injury. Expulsion. Fire drill. The principal sends you home for forging your father's signature on your report card.

This is Toronto.

Shift. The past. BAHT and her father are seated in his car, not speaking, staring forward. FATHER is lost in thought, perplexed. BAHT is scared.

Are you mad, Bah Bah?

FATHER   Yes.

BAHT   Because the principal sent me home?

FATHER   No.

BAHT   Because I forged your signature?

FATHER   No. Because you got caught. Now, take this pen and practise. Go on, practise. Here's how I sign my name.

She makes a signature in the air and points out the etymology of it.

Notice the arc in the first bridge of the "M," and how the tail of the "P" dips down beneath the other letters. The "S," here, hooks in to the cage of the

4

"R." Bold strokes. Confidence. Don't *construct* the signature, let the signature construct itself.

She practises.

Don't ever get sent home again, Baht. Your reputation starts now. And we have nothing—*nothing*—if we do not have our reputation. Even if you get caught, there are other ways out. You just have to be creative. Can you be creative?

BAHT holds up a sample of his forged signature.

BAHT   How's that?

FATHER   *(smiles)* Yes. Yes, you're going to be just fine.

Shift.

BAHT   There are six choices you have when you turn eighteen. Go to university. Travel the world. Get married to your high-school sweetheart. Join the family business. Join the family business. Join the family business.

BAHT lights another incense stick. Two now burn.

This is Montreal.

The light snaps off. There is fire, smoke and sirens. Counterfeit money is everywhere; BAHT is stuffing as much as she can into a duffle bag. She calls out to her FATHER.

Bah! *(beat)* Bah! *(beat)* Dad, they're here, they're here… come on, Dad! We have to go. They're playing our song, let's go.

She stops and looks at her FATHER.

Bah? What are you doing? Why are you burning the money? Dad, that's the *job*, don't burn the—

FATHER   Go.

BAHT   C'mon, Dad.

FATHER   Go, Baht.

BAHT   I'm not leaving you. Let's go before the fire takes out our exit.

FATHER   Leave me, Baht. I will go out through the front door.

BAHT   There are *cops* out the front door.

FATHER   I know.

BAHT   The basement's our exit, we go—

FATHER   I am going out through the front door.

He starts towards the door.

BAHT   Dad! *Dad!*

A rush of flames. He is gone. Gunshots. Another rush of flames. BAHT takes the basement. Shift. BAHT turns the light bulb back on.

I waited for six days at the hotel for you.

She lights another incense stick. Three now burn.

This is Quebec City.

Shift. Quebec City. BAHT is on the phone, pacing and smoking.

Tommy. It's Baht. My father is dead. He's got to be.
It's been six days. If he had a pulse, he'd be here. *(beat)*
I'm getting outta town a bit, let things cool here.
Look, Tommy, the job, the Russian job… it burned.
He burned it before the cops— So, if they come
around, the Russians… I'm gonna get disappeared.

7

Tell them what you have to, but give me a head start. *(beat)* Thanks, Tommy. I'll see you around.

BAHT turns the light back on.

This is Las Vegas.

She lights another incense stick. Four now burn.

Shift. She is in a temple. She takes the money from the duffle bag and throws six bills into the pyre. She smiles at the other people and waits for them to leave. She looks around carefully. She takes out a cigarette and lights it from the flame.

Hi Bah. Finally in Vegas. It's... hot. And bright.

She burns six more bills.

I brought you some Hell money. Twenty large. It's, uh... it's mostly fake. I was practising on the bus ride over. I think I got it perfect now. Here... check those out.

Beat. She takes a long drag and exhales.

I haven't been sleeping. It's hard here. This place is so full of sin and sound. There's a slot machine in my bathroom, and a guy outside singing "Blue Moon" in perfect Cantonese. *(beat)* The job in Montreal, the Russian job… they found me.

Shift.

RUSSIAN   Psst. Hey, girl. Over here. Climb in. *(She does.)* Hello. You are girl with number for first name, da? We deal with your father for job in Montreal. He supposed to call, no call. We wait, it's okay, understand… six days! Niet. No call. We reading there big fire following police raiding Chinese lab. We think "Oh no," terrible news. But wait… look outside, see girl with number for first name boarding bus to Las Vegas. Thank God, she is okay. *(beat)* You may have heard Russians, we are not so good people. Russian and Chinese especially, long history, not so nice. But we are good people. We have the sympathetic feelings. People die, it is tragic, we are sad. But still is leaving us with no money. So we make decision. You will get us the money. Six weeks. Father had golden reputation. You keep his promise, da? You make bill that will pass the Burn Test. *(beat)* And no one else has to die.

Shift.

BAHT   There are six tests to prove the authenticity of a legal tender banknote. The Holograph Test. The Ultraviolet Test. The Watermark Test. The Security Thread Test. The Intaglio Test. *(beat)* And the Burn Test.

BAHT turns the light back on.

This is Los Angeles.

She lights another incense stick. Five now burn.

BAHT is in another temple, this one in downtown LA. It is Qingming.

Happy Qingming, Bah.

She burns six bills.

I have two weeks before the deadline with the Russians and I'm nowhere near done. Bah, did you really promise these guys a bill that would pass the Burn Test? Bah, I can't do it. No one can do it. I... I didn't even think *you* could do it. And you were the best. You told me when I was a kid that you could fake the sunset if you wanted to. I never trusted the damn thing again. Bah, even if I print on a legit linen paper, the flame emission doesn't pass on account of the ink. If I boost the ink, the intaglio fails. And if I do it all to pass, Bah, the whole goddamn process is too expensive!

I went back to the plans for Montreal. I don't get it, Dad. The way we were hanging paper you'd think it was all figured out. But the paper was wrong, the ink was wrong... it all *looked* great, but it wasn't proof. It wasn't real. *(beat)* And it wouldn't have passed the Burn Test.

So what the hell were we doing?

Beat.

My time is up. Someone has to pay; they're gonna *make* someone pay for this. And wherever I run...

Beat. She looks at the Hell money in her hand. Looks at the fire. She holds the bills over the pyre. She drops the entire load of bills into the fire.

Shift.

There are six documents you need in order to start a new life, with a new identity. A birth certificate. A driver's licence. A social insurance number. A health card. A passport. A credit card.

11

She turns the light back on.

This is Vancouver.

She lights another incense stick. Six now burn.

I call the Russians and set the meet. Ten p.m., ware-house district. When they arrive I hand them masks. "The press oil gets hot and the vapours are highly toxic."

I line up the suitcases. They're expecting more.

I don't have it. The fire in Montreal. My father died. I couldn't complete the job. *(She waves at the cases.)* There's your money back.

RUSSIAN   You little bitch—you say you could do job.

BAHT   I appreciate you didn't get the work you asked for, I can give you the names of some available cooks in the city, one of them could help you…

RUSSIAN   No! No one can "help me"! I need perfect bills, nowhere can I get perfect bills. Your reputation is shit now… you might want to learn skill trade like

bicycle fixing, because you have no credit in the
Eastern bloc as of now.

BAHT   And that's when I really understood what you did.
And that's when I really understood what I had to do.
You never got it, Bah. You never passed the Burn Test.
You staked your reputation on this thing and it was
a wash. That's why you lit the place up at the raid.
And that's why you went out the front door. You son
of a bitch. You put your reputation before your life.
Before me. 'Cause it's better to die the best hanger in
the Western world than to live with tarnished credit.
And I get it. I get it because I'm there now, I'm you
now… and I'm telling you I understand.

But you're still a son of a bitch.

Beat.

The Russians start arguing. I start making for the
door. The one to the left gets antsy, he tears off his
mask.

Shift.

Six steps to the door.

Shift.

He throws the mask on the floor and takes a deep breath in. He stops and looks around. He can smell it now.

Shift.

Six yards to the car.

Shift.

The maskless guy starts yelling at the others in Russian. Presumably to tell them about the gasoline he smells. The puddle of it they're standing in.

Shift.

Six documents in the car.

Shift.

Meanwhile one of them checks the bills and runs his fingers over the intaglio on the face of the first. A bit of it smears off. They're piecing it together.

Shift.

Six minutes to the airport.

Shift.

I hear the slide of a 9mm snap back as I spark the
lighter in my right hand. It drops as I lock the office
door behind me.

A rush of fire. Gunshots. Another rush of fire.

And I go out the front door.

She snuffs out all six incense sticks.

This is somewhere far, far away.

Blackout.

PAPER cuts

HOPE is writing at a desk. There is a wastebasket filled with crumpled-up paper beside her. She stops writing, looks critically at the paper, crumples it and throws it into the wastebasket. She begins anew with another paper.

HOPE   I can't begin this. I can't begin this. I can't…

            Dear John. I know this will come as quite a shock
            to you. I know you really thought this would last,

that this would be the one to... last. I know there's nothing I can say that will...

Fuck, I know everything except *(She crumples the paper.)* how to begin this.

She begins again on another paper.

Dear John. I hate you. I've always hated you, I think, it's just that it took until now to realize it. I hated you when I met you. I hated you on our first date when we rented that movie with Joe Piscopo. I hated you when I met your parents. I hated your parents for *having* you. I hate every single one of your do-nothing, pot-smoking, zero-ambition friends. I hate the apartment you live in. I hate all the furniture and the carpet and... well, the tile in the kitchen is nice, it's more of a warm... but I hate everything else. I hate that you don't smoke and don't drink and don't miss me when I'm away. I hate that you call my parents by their first names. And I really, John, I *really* hate your fucking cat. I've hated these things for the entire year and three months we've been dating, and the previous two months when we were just fucking. I hated them then, John, just *imagine* how deeply rooted my hate is *now*. In closing, fuck you. Love, Hope. P.S. Hate Hate Hate.

17

Pause.

Fuck.

She crumples the paper and starts another.

Dear John. It's not you, it's me. Just kidding, it's you.

She crumples the paper and starts another.

Dear John.

Pause, she crumples and starts another.

Dear John.

Pause, then another.

Dear John.

Pause, then another.

Dear Scott. I know your name isn't "Scott," but it all just seems so cliché writing a "Dear John" letter to someone *actually* named John.

Pause.

Fuck.

She crumples the paper and starts another.

Dear John. I'm gay.

She crumples the paper and begins another letter.

Dear John. *(beat)* You're gay.

She crumples the paper and begins another.

Dear John. They say in group… *(She begins to say "therapy" but changes to:)* discussion that you should write a list of things you'd like to change about your relationship. Here is the list of things I think need changed in our relationship: Number one: You. End of list. Love, Hope.

She crumples the paper and starts another.

Dear John. By the time you read this, I will be gone.

She crumples the paper and starts again.

Dear John. By the time you read this, I will be...
not here. I will always cherish our time together,
and carry your memory in my heart like a whisper
of times gone by. My heart seeks to fly free like a
dove unburdened and—

She crumples the paper and starts another.

Dear John. We have your girlfriend. Deliver
$500,000 in unmarked bills to locker #91 at the
bus terminal by midnight or you'll never see her
again. We are a group of international terrorists and
should be taken very, very seriously. We mean it. If
you go to the police, you won't see your girlfriend
again. Actually, in all likelihood, you won't see her
again anyway. So you may as well save yourself the
$500,000 and just forget this ever happened. We'll
find the money eventually and everyone will be happy. Except maybe you. Best of luck in all your future
endeavours. Love, Nameless Group of International
Terrorists.

Pause. She shakes her head, crumples the paper and starts another.

Dear John. This is my thirty-fourth letter to you, and
I still don't know what to say. I'm not the writer,
John, I'm not the one whose words are their stock

in trade, that's not me. You were the artist, I was the accountant, and we lived like that, that's who we were. We were happy. I was happy. I swear. But now I'm not. Because…

(aside) Why? Why aren't I happy…?

(back to the letter) I'm not happy because… because feelings change, John, I don't know. How do I explain this? Sometimes you just don't feel things you used to feel and every fucking thing you do gets on my nerves and one day I wake up to the unbearable fact that you snore and drool in your sleep and that used to be cute but now it's just fucking annoying 'cause how would you feel if *you* woke up in a puddle of drool, and I guess you do know but it's different, 'cause it's *your* drool, and it's just annoying how you used to be so in love with me and I used to be so in love with you but now we're just going through the motions of something that used to be something good but it's not something good anymore it's just this blob of "something" that used to be something else. *(Pause; she's out of breath.)* And now I have to rewrite this 'cause I know how you get about run-on sentences.

She crumples the paper and starts another.

21

Dear John. We had some good times. And it's important that you understand, I remember them all. Everywhere I look in this city, I see our footprints. Truth be told, I didn't really like you when we first met. But, oh, how I grew to love you, John. I grew to love you so much it was terrible and frightening. And you know it was frightening, 'cause you'd find me sometimes in the bathroom, sitting in the tub, running water and just *crying* because it was so fucking scary how in love with you I was. How every day you had to convince me that, yeah, it really was *me* you wanted to be with. So this... maybe this is just one of those times. Right? I think I'm going to leave, I think you don't love me, but you do. I'm sorry. I won't...

She pauses, over-emotional. She looks at the paper, takes a deep breath and crumples it up. She gasps and draws her hand back. She got a paper cut.

Ow, fuck.

She shakes her hand, sucks on the cut, blows on it, then shakes her hand around again while silently cursing. She takes another piece of paper and stares at it. She now writes slowly, carefully.

Dear John. I… have… a paper cut. I have a paper cut. It's… small. And it's thin. So thin there's no blood. So thin you'd miss it, even if you looked real hard. It's this tiny little paper cut, and if you did manage to look at it, you'd say it was inconsequential. I'd ask you for a bandage but you'd say it wouldn't make a difference either way. And… and that's why I can't show it to you. Why I never showed it to you. 'Cause it's small. And it's thin. And there's not even any blood. *(Pause. She is painfully sincere.)* But it hurts. It hurts so deep and so bad and… sometimes, at night, I'd search you all over. I'd search your skin, every pore and crease… to see if you had one too. But you're perfect, John. You're impenetrable.

I'm sorry. I'm so sorry. Love, Hope.

She stops writing, laying the pen across the page. She gets up, slowly, and walks off.

PAPER dolls

We are in MUTT's bedroom. MUTT is a girl of about eight years. She has a plethora of stuffed animals in her room, propped up as an audience, and a small cut-out cardboard box on a stand that serves for putting on puppet shows. There is a small table next to it that has several sheets of paper, markers, scissors and other various items lying on it. MUTT comes in, slamming the door behind her and yelling defiantly:

MUTT   *Well I don't even like your dinner, so BLEH!*

She sits down at the table and scowls, then sets to work cutting crude figures out of paper. She stands them up, two crude puppets, one male and one female.

> *(as female)* Blah blah blah me me me...

> *(as male)* Blah blah blah you you you...

> *(as both)* GO TO YOUR ROOM FOR NO REASON! NO DINNER! *(pause)* Blah!

MUTT looks up at the audience of stuffed animals.

> My new parents. The Blahs. *(indicates the female)* Mrs. Blah. *(indicates the male)* And Mr. Blah. *(Deviously, she picks up a marker and draws on Mr. Blah's face.)* Mr. Blah has one big eyebrow instead of two. He wears big ugly glasses and smells like envelopes. *(She draws Mrs. Blah.)* Mrs. Blah has big fake boobs and looks kind of like a racoon.

She picks up the scissors and waves them towards the Blahs.

> *(as the Blahs)* Noooooooooo!!!!!!!!!!!

She snips their heads off and happily discards the bodies.

I heard them talking. They're going to give me back in the morning. This is my fifth family this year. Sister Sheila says God is punishing me. She says that's what God does to people like me. Mutts. She says that this is what happens when people cross-breed coloured people and white people. *(pause)* No one wants us. Sister Sheila says if I was one or the other, then I'd find a family. Mutts just get traded like baseball cards.

MUTT sits at the desk and searches for something. She can't find it. She does another tour of the room but comes up empty. She looks at her stuffed animal audience.

Have you guys seen my real parents? *(pause)* The Blahs threw them out, didn't they? *(pause)* Yeah, thought so. Oh well. We can make them again.

She takes some paper and scissors and goes to work. She cuts two paper figures and starts colouring them in, narrating as she goes.

My father was Scottish. Scottish people play soccer, but they call it football, and eat things like sheep guts.

She continues making the figures.

They drink lots of beer and talk with funny accents.

She completes her FATHER. Continues making her mother.

> Mom was "Oriental." They all eat rice and talk with funny accents and are very very polite and good at math.

She finishes making her MOTHER.

> Hi guys.

FATHER   Right, hallo, wee lassie!

MOTHER   Konnichi-wa. Ne ho mah!

She looks at her paper parents with pleasure, and a little bit of sadness.

MUTT   I never met them. But I think they looked like this. *(pause)* I miss you guys.

MOTHER   *(weakly)* We missing you too…

MUTT is despondent.

MUTT   Forget it…

She folds her arms and lays her head down. Her parents are now on either side of her.

MOTHER   She sounding upset.

FATHER   Poor lass.

MOTHER   She grow up be so pretty.

FATHER   *(flirtatious)* Aye, just like her mother.

MOTHER   *(laughs timidly... actually, everything she does is timid)*
              Oh, stop... *leng jai-ah.*

They kiss, MOTHER *squeals... timidly.*

FATHER   Shhh. You'll wake her up!

MUTT   I'm not sleeping. Are you guys coming back soon?

FATHER   We're here now, lass.

MUTT   But the real you. The one without a Popsicle stick
              holding you up. Can you come get me? I hate it
              here.

MOTHER   You need cheering up. I make you some congee.

MUTT   What's congee?

MOTHER   *(shocked)* What? No one ever make you congee! What sort of place you live in?

FATHER   Calm down, missus. She dinnae need porridge anyway. I can cheer her up with my remarkable Sean Connery impression. *(imitates Sean Connery)* Mishter Goldfinger, I preshume.

He looks to MOTHER *and* MUTT *for approval.*

           Eh? Eh?

MUTT   Who's Sean Connery?

FATHER   *(enraged) What*!?! You don't know who Sean Connery is? Unacceptable!

MOTHER   Now who getting upset?

FATHER   But it's *Sean Connery*! He's a cultural institution!

MOTHER   So is congee.

FATHER   Now you look here—

MUTT   Stop it! I'm sorry I don't know about congee or Sean Connery, okay? I'm just a stupid mutt.

MOTHER *(sotto)* Now look what you did.

FATHER I'm sorry. *(They kiss. Then, to MUTT:)* Right then, who called you a mutt?

MUTT Sister Sheila does. The other kids at the orphanage. They say no one wants a stupid half-breed.

MOTHER What else did evil sister tell you?

MUTT She said that you're dead 'cause God punished you for making me. You guys were planning to have more mutt children and take over the world, so God struck you down with lightning.

MOTHER What? No no no ... we were not struck by lightning, daughter. We were struck by Toyota Prius!

MUTT What?

MOTHER Ironic, I know...

FATHER Ach, it's true, lass. Here's what happened: Once upon a time. There was a lad and a lass named Father and Mother. When they met, they knew they were meant for one another. And one day they had a daughter... *(a paper doll of MUTT as a newborn pops up)* who

30

they named Daughter… They lived in a lovely house in the Annex.

MUTT cuts them a house, then puts it inside the theatre. The dolls stand in front of it. MUTT is now the puppet master, behind the theatre, her head peering over.

MOTHER I remember it bigger…

FATHER *(chiding)* It's a bonnie house.

MOTHER So Mother, Father and Daughter live in this lovely, but slightly cramped, house and are very happy together. You even had a puppy. He was mix breed, just like you.

MUTT A mutt.

MOTHER No, not "mutt." Mix breed. Half and half. All the house was half and half. We have half one table, half another table, nail together, one kitchen table. Half of Mother's and half of Father's belongings all put together to make most original and beautiful house. Just like Daughter.

FATHER One afternoon, when Daughter was only one year old, we went out for groceries in the car. *(MUTT makes them a car and they get in.)* Mother and Father in the front, Daughter in the child seat in the back. We were halfway between the Asian grocery store and the Scottish bakery when it hit us.

Another paper car pops up and smashes into their car.

MOTHER Another car come, crash right into us! Aiyah! Father and Mother both perish. But Daughter, is miracle, still alive! Not one scratch!

FATHER Aye. The next thing we know, there's this bright light *(MUTT shines a flashlight on them.)* and this big silver cloud appears *(A big silver cloud appears.)* and a voice says:

GOD Oy! You there!

FATHER It was God!

MUTT God is Scottish?

FATHER Yer damn right he is.

GOD Oy! Yer dead. Right, on yer bike, le's go, jimmy, line forms over 'ere.

32

MOTHER   But we couldn't go.

GOD   C'mon now, yer 'oldin up traffic.

FATHER   God. If I may call you God.

GOD   Me mates call me Angus.

MOTHER   We say: Angus! Please! We cannot leave Daughter. She is all alone. Who will care for her?

GOD   Well I cannae sen' ye bach. The lass dinnae ha' aunties or uncles?

MOTHER   No. She has no one but us.

GOD   Well load o' good tha' does her, yer dead!

FATHER   Please, Angus, can we no work something out?

GOD   Ach. A'right, ye daft humans.

MOTHER   And so, we all sat down and worked out a deal.

Contracts appear in their hands and they work over the details.

GOD   Okay, so I let ye stay and watch o'er her until she's... ten.

MOTHER   Thirty.

GOD   Fifteen.

MOTHER   Forty-two.

GOD   Twenty.

MOTHER   Deal. And we get to see her whenever we want. And protect her from bad people. And she go to college of her choice.

GOD   Okay okay okay! Anything else? Divine powers? Ability to turn water into wine?

MOTHER   She not drink. Turn her all red.

GOD   Now, in return... Father, ye'll play fer oor football league. We ha' tournies ev'ry Saturday against the Rangers.

FATHER   Magic.

GOD   And Mother...

MOTHER   I watch over Daughter. That full-time job.

GOD   A'right, then. Y'know, I dinnae see a lot of parents who love a child so much. We're about finished 'ere. I haveta get bach upstairs. Cheerio.

MOTHER   Angus! *(beat)* Daughter. She will be okay, ne?

GOD   Ach. Dinnae fache yersel, lass. She'll be just fine. *(With that, the cloud disappears.)*

MUTT   Wow.

FATHER   Aye. We got you a good deal, lass.

MOTHER   Go to sleep now, Daughter. We make sure nothing bad happen.

FATHER   We'll be right here, watchin' over ye.

MUTT   I love you guys.

MOTHER   We love you too, Daughter. Now go sleep, or you get wrinkles when you're older.

MUTT   Okay. Good night.

MUTT goes to her bed, taking the dolls with her. She lays on her back and holds her parents up at her chest.

MOTHER   Goodnight, Daughter.

FATHER   Goodnight, sweet girl.

MUTT closes her eyes.

(yawning) I'm a bit tuckered out m'self. Care to join me in the boudoir?

MOTHER   *(giggling)* She will hear us! We traumatize her!

FATHER   Ach, she'll be fine. C'mon now…

They giggle as they disappear out of MUTT's sight.

PAPER tears

WISDOM enters and sits at a long table. He is at a job interview.

WISDOM   Hi. I think I'm your nine o'clock... my name's
            Wisdom. *(pause)* Have I had any... yes, The Dragon
            Inn, a Chinese... *(pause)* I had to leave—well, the
            whole staff, really, had to... it's kind of a funny
            story.

*Shift. The Dragon Inn. The scene plays out with WISDOM at times nar-
rating and participating in the action.*

I was waiting this table, and the girl seemed really nice, cute in a naive kind of way, and the guy seemed decent. They talked about ordinary things, the guy mentioned only having a few first dates since his girlfriend dumped him (I can hear this, 'cause it's a small restaurant and I'm a very adept eavesdropper). I take their order, send it back to the kitchen, King brings their food. King works the back because he's got some mental issues. Watched *God of Gamblers* too many times, carries a deck of cards and a Glock 17 with him everywhere. So he brings their food, they eat, I do my job... go in to check the bathrooms... and then the guy comes in. He's on his cellphone, having this real easy conversation while pissing in the urinal:

MAN   Yeah, I'm stuck here at work, gonna be pretty late. Tell him that he doesn't get dessert if he doesn't do the dishes. Just a phase...

WISDOM   He finishes up and takes a wedding ring out of his pants pocket and slips it into a fold in his wallet, then takes a condom out of the same fold and puts it in his pants pocket. Straight trade.

MAN   I love you too, sweet dreams.

WISDOM   He hangs up the phone, checks his hair. Then, get this, motherfucker winks at me before he leaves. Like one of those *I won't tell if you won't* winks. Now, I'm not a moral high-horse kinda guy. Truth is, I don't give a fuck what you do as long as you don't do it to me. But something about that wink just pissed me off.

They call for the bill, and it hits me. I take two fortune cookies out of their wrappers and remove the fortune from one of them. Ripping the corner off an old order form, I write a new fortune on it, something a little more personal than "Good luck and prosperity will find you in the new year," slip it back in the cookie and send them over with our other waiter, Love. Love slept with a girl I had a crush on for years, so if anyone was going to get hurt over this, I wanted it to be him.

The man reads his first:

MAN   You will find luck, good fortune and change… In bed…

WISDOM   I fuckin' hate that joke.

MAN   What does yours say?

WISDOM   The girl unfolds her fortune. Her face goes from sunny to overcast in a heartbeat.

GIRL   He has a wedding ring in his wallet…

WISDOM   They leave, silent and separately. As the man walks out the front door, Calm (the host) brings him a two-for-one coupon.

CALM   Perhaps your wife would like to try our fortune cookies as well.

WISDOM   We did a good thing. Really. *(beat)* Of course, four single and lonely guys in their early twenties could hardly harness this newfound power. We abused it some, played some pretty nasty tricks, pissed off a lot of people. We had no sense of fiscal responsibility, so less business just meant more time for King to beat us in mah-jong in the back room. Funny thing was… we didn't get less business. We got *more* business. Word got out that the Dragon Inn had the most original and uncanny fortune cookies, and customers flocked by the dozen. A few weeks after that first time, we had to adjust our staffing so it was just one guy working the front and three guys in the back furiously writing fortunes.

Depending on who was writing your fortune, every customer got a personal spin on their future. Calm wrote Zen-like passages about tranquillity and rivers: "The mind springs from hidden depths of oceans past and present." Love would have the most balls-out statements, including: "You're ugly" and "Next time I'll nibble your dumplings, call me." King took it the most seriously out of all of us. He really thought he could tell their future… for a while King thought he was psychic. Then again, for a while, King thought he was Chow Yun-Fat, but that's neither here nor there. I tried to keep to my original MO: eavesdrop and give good advice. So I feel that my missives of: "Look at his car, he's compensating for something" and "Weren't you here last night with a different guy, you slut," were totally justified.

We were just having fun. That's all.

Until one night.

I'm cleaning dishes in the back, scraping bits of jiaozi off a plate, when there's this loud crash in the dining area, and Calm runs through the kitchen, grabs me hard by the shoulder and drags me to table twelve, where Love is facing off with some guy.

What the fuck is going on?

CALM   Love, man. Love wrote his girlfriend a fortune.

WISDOM   What did he write?

CALM   Motherfucker wrote, "You want a real man, call me" on her fucking cookie. Only she didn't get it… *(He points.)* He did.

WISDOM   I take a second to look closer at the guy and now I know why Calm's so… not Calm. The guy's tattooed, Big Circle. Triad. *(to CALM)* "Oh, fuck."

            Love's obviously not seeing something, he's stepped right up in the guy's face, doesn't know to lay off, the guy's fucking *marked*. Poor kid's blinded by love or rage or just caught being twenty years old on the wrong day, in the wrong situation. A little bit older, a little bit wiser, maybe we could've… but we didn't.

            Big Circle rolls deep, and suddenly there's another thug closing in on Love. Calm jumps ship to the front desk, leaves me standing alone in the middle of the floor. And maybe I was blinded by something too. Ideals. Hope. Being twenty. I really thought we could just… work it out.

Then it all went to hell. 'Cause the one guy you don't want around in a potentially explosive situation… is the God of fucking gamblers.

King rushes outta the backroom with some kinda war cry, sweeping up his apron to reveal the Glock tucked into the waistband of his pants. Motherfucker actually did a dive roll over someone's table, like that scene in *Hard Boiled*. It was so ridiculous it was almost cool.

He comes out of his roll, the Glock out and aimed at the Triad's head. The tattoos both reach, and now Triad has a Beretta at Love's head, and his thug's got a bead on King with a *laser-sighted* Smith & Wesson. And if *that* weren't enough of a standoff, in strolls fucking Calm, cocking the store shotgun we keep under the front desk. Thug responds with *another* piece, now double-fisting: one on King, one on Calm.

Five guys, five guns, if everybody shoots, nobody lives. It's a Mexican standoff in a Chinese restaurant. And all I want to do is wash dishes.

I figure I gotta say something profound and shit, like "Stop the violence," but all that comes out is: "Dude, what the fuck? It's just a girl. She's just another girl." It seems to work. Their guns waiver,

Love is sweating buckets, but Triad's gun is slowly moving down. "Okay," I say, "I'm going to go into the kitchen now. I'm going to do the dishes. And if this mess isn't gone by the time I'm done, I'm gonna call the police."

With that, I turn my back and head for the kitchen.

I'd swear it was one shot. Just as I reached the kitchen door. One shot. Then five bodies all fell to the ground at once. I didn't dare turn around. I went back into the kitchen. I finished the dishes. And then I called the police. The papers called it a "massacre." Soon the story of the fortune cookie got out and they were all over it: "Five Slain Over Fortune Cookie Love Letter."

It's wrong though. It wasn't because of a fortune cookie. I stand by that. Truth is, tiny fortunes written on paper... they make the world go round. But love... love almost always ends in gunplay.

So... to answer your question: Yes. I have had some restaurant experience.

PAPER folds|sbloł ЯƎꟼAꟼ

SYMBOL *is in his living room. He is breaking up with his girlfriend.*

SYMBOL   I didn't kiss you. Once. And it was... what, it was...
months ago! You can't... I mean, that's just fucking
absurd to throw... all of this, for one time I didn't
kiss you? Okay, okay, then this, answer this... is it
that I didn't kiss you, or that I didn't tell you why?
Which are you mad at, then, which... why am I
even discussing this? It's not important, not the is-
sue, not the heart of things, how can *one kiss* be...
the heart of things?

It's not, it never is. One thing is never... and we say it is, we always *say* it is, but it's *not*. That's so, that's movie magic and romantic John fucking Hughes tells you that it's that one thing, that one thing can change everything. But it can't. You just watch too many movies.

A relationship, like ours, like our... *relationship*... it's more complex than that. Paper folds. *(beat)* You don't remember that. *(beat)* It was when we first met. You were at a bar. So was I. The same bar, that just makes sense.

Shift. He is at the bar.

Hi. Hi. I saw you from over... I'm sitting just over there. And I saw you. *(pause)* My name's Symbol. *(pause)* Yeah, like a literary device, not a *(He mimes a rimshot.)* Symbol. *(Pause, he looks at his hands.)* This? Oh, it's... a crane. I think. I think that's what they're called. *(slight pause)* Origami, yeah. The napkins here are good for that. Paper folds. *(pause)* I get nervous, sometimes, and I fold... I used to smoke, now I make cranes. *(pause)* And I'm nervous... I guess 'cause I don't usually come up to people at bars... or... anywhere. So I was sitting there, over where I was sitting, and I wrote my number down for you, on my napkin. But I got nervous, watching you, and… well… *(He presents the crane.)* It's inside. If you'd like to call, it's my cell number. And if you don't… well… now you have a pet crane.

Shift. He is back in the present.

You remember now. *(beat)* But you still don't understand.

He holds up a sheet of paper.

This. This is us. *(He takes another sheet of paper.)* So is this. *(another piece)* Us. *(another piece)* Us. Everyone. This, it's a fucking… canvas. For everyone; writer, poet, painter, it's potential. But it's not a novel. And it's not a poem. It's not a mural. And it's not a relationship. You think one kiss can do or undo everything in the past year?

He folds one sheet of paper down the middle.

This is one kiss.

He sets the paper aside and picks up another one. He makes an identical fold down the middle.

One kiss. Maybe the first. *(another fold)* The second. *(another fold)* The first time we slept together. *(another fold)* The first time we slept together fully naked. *(another)* Breakfast the first morning we woke up still together. *(another)* Our first fight. *(another)* Meeting my parents. *(another)* The week we spent in Hawaii, getting lost in Waikiki. *(another)* The first time we shared a toothbrush. *(another)* The time I got jealous about your ex and threatened to leave. *(another)* All those times we stayed up till morning smoking cigarettes on your balcony, *(another)* and all the times we got caught in the rain. *(another)* The restaurant we used to eat at, *(another)* when you called it "our table" and I smiled. *(another)* Bowls of cereal and lazy Saturday mornings. *(another)* All the good. *(another)* All the bad.

One last fold, and he presents an origami crane.

This is a relationship.

He holds up the first sheet of paper with one fold made in it.

This is one kiss. *(beat)* Do you understand now? Paper folds. That's all it is.

Christ, it was one kiss. Just let it go. After all I've done for you. Just let this go. I need to hold on to something. *(pause)* This isn't about winning. It's not about being right. And it's not—it's not about getting your way, how I always let you get your way. Each time I folded in half, then thirds, then quarters for you. And it was never enough. My hair was either too long or too short. My shoes too scuffed or too shiny. Either too uncultured, or trying to put on airs. For every change I made, it was just as much wrong as it was right. And the only thing for certain was that I was no longer the person I used to be. If he walked in the room right now, I wouldn't know him from Adam. You were everything to me. And I spent every day and every dollar to manufacture myself… so I could be everything to you.

You took me like a sheet of paper. You folded and creased me where you needed lenience. You tore me when I was uneven. You shaped me and unshaped me, until I became too worn. And now I stand here, formless and tattered… because you couldn't decide what you wanted to make.

So if you want to do it this way, your way, one last time, we'll do that. But it's for good. I'll tell you.

I'll tell you why I didn't kiss you that day, if that's what you need to hear. I'll do that for you. And then I'll leave, and say "Have a nice life." Or. You can take my hand, right now. You can take my hand, and tell me everything's going to be okay, and I'll believe you... and none of this will have ever happened.

He extends his hand.

What's it going to be?

He waits for several beats. He slowly withdraws his hand and takes a deep breath. Pause.

It was that day, we were meeting for lunch. Eaton Centre, the Queen Street entrance. I was late. Came in the wrong entrance, and I saw you waiting. Your back was to me, and you were waiting, looking out by the door for me. You were leaning against a pillar. Waiting, right? 'Cause I'm late, I was always so late. I stood there, right behind you... and just *watched* you. For what... oh God, it felt like so long, for... I don't know, minutes, I guess, but it felt... days. Could've been days. I watched the way you brushed your hair over your left ear when you got impatient. The way your foot scuffed the floor. The way you leaned, shifted your weight from foot to foot and back. Everything. I memorized you. Finally, I came up behind you, slid my hands around your waist. You turned, and this part you remember... You leaned in and tried to kiss me, but I pulled away. *(pause)* I pulled away... because I didn't want to close my eyes.

He takes the origami crane in hand.

After I leave, you'll unfold this, and you'll look for a phone number. An address, something. You won't find one. And even though I told you that, I know you'll still unfold it once I'm gone. That's just who you are. And knowing that... I guess that's how I know I love you. *(pause)* I love you.

He places the crane in front of him.

Have a nice life.

He exits.

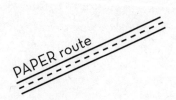

PAPER route

A taxicab in downtown Toronto. A passenger enters and mumbles a destination to ISAAC, the cab driver. The passenger notices where ISAAC's hack papers (taxi licence) should be, there is another licence in its place: a medical school diploma. ISAAC looks at the passenger in his rear-view.

ISAAC   Funny how a degree in one country looks different from that in another.

He points to the diploma.

This is from AIIMS in New Delhi. It certifies me as a medical doctor, specializing in the kidney and liver. When I was eight, my youngest sister died of liver disease… and the kidney, well the kidney just makes you lots of money if you know what to do with it. Fifteen years, including residency.

He holds up the hack lying on the seat next to him.

This is from the Effective Taxicab Driver Training Program run by the City of Toronto MLS Training Section, which I attended when I arrived in Canada. It is a seventeen-day course, preparing me to meet the challenges and demands of my new job. Yes, everything from professional customer service to effective business management, in a concise three-week course.

This is my class:

Sahiv, he is from my old neighbourhood.

SAHIV   Isaac used to beat me up…

ISAAC   Sammy and Pinhead are from Mumbai and Nagpur, respectively.

PINHEAD   I hate being called Pinhead, I want a new nickname.

SAMMY   Shut up, Pinhead.

ISAAC   And then, there is Mr. X.

MR. X   White people can't say my name properly. Just call me Mr. X. Simpler.

ISAAC   Together, we form a Bollywood dance troupe and win over our white supervisors with our whimsical songs and amusing cultural idiosyncrasies. We pinwheel out of the classroom and perform a rousing little number on the hoods of our new taxis called "Toronto Nights, Bombay Dreams." Would you like to see it?

He starts to do a few graceful arm motions, then stops.

I'm kidding. No, my class was not an Aishwarya Rai movie. Sahiv has an advanced degree in biochemistry, while Mr. X is a pathologist. Pinhead and Sammy are general physicians, though Pinhead did take advanced neurobiology at AIIMS.

We all came to Canada with papers much like this one. Some of them in frames, some folded carefully

and placed neatly in a box, some kept at all times—
like mine—in a bag. A doctor's bag, like the ones
in the movies. This was my first gift, from my wife,
when I started my residency.

MEERA   It is like the one Mandy Patinkin has on *Chicago Hope*
in the episode entitled "An Apple A Day." You are
my Mandy Patinkin.

ISAAC   To think, if she had just switched channels, I could
have been George Clooney.

I'm digressing.

Out of school, we are employed by general taxi
services, except for Sahiv, who is driving airport
limousines. At seven each evening, when rush hour
is just finishing, we order takeout from the deli
on Gerrard. We park our cabs in empty lots, sit
on our hoods, pass around Thumbs Up and cigarettes… talk about our days, gossip about our fares,
bitch about the state of the world. It's like an episode of *Desperate Housewives*, but with brown guys.
Desperate Indians.

MR. X   Another ticket, Isaac? Another? You idiot. This is
what happens when you cheat on your driver's test.

ISAAC   I didn't cheat, for the last time!

MR. X   You copied off Sahiv, I saw you!

ISAAC   Bakwas! You cheated in school. Medical school! That's worse!

MR. X   I told you that in confidence, bastard! *(He laughs.)* It wasn't cheating, not technically. *(sighs, explains to the other men)* Okay, in my last year of school, I opened an underground free clinic in Faridabad. The people there, we walk by them every day, but no one helps. I wanted to help. A sixteen-year-old girl came to me, she was pregnant and needed desperately to terminate. She had been raped. I helped her. She turned out to be Professor Verma's daughter. At the time I was failing biomedical ethics. The next week, I had an A.

ISAAC   The night he told us that, he and I stayed up until sunrise, drinking beer on his porch.

MR. X   I haven't thought about that in years: the free clinic, helping people. I haven't helped anyone in four years, Isaac.

ISAAC   Why do you stay?

MR. X   This city is sick, my friend. It grows sicker by the day. India, it is sick too. But I think I can help this place, Isaac. It just has to let me. There's a cure in me. I am the cure to something, here. I believe that.

ISAAC   And he did. He does. X is a doctor. He could never be anything else.

However, that was the last time I heard X speak that way. In the following weeks, I begin to see something in X I cannot quite diagnose. For a pathologist, he smokes more than any of us, and he always looks as if he hasn't slept for days. But I think what really worries me is how the light, the hope, has faded from his eyes.

Sahiv, man… I had this fare this morning, this Indian girl, she was *smoking* hot, yaar.

SAHIV   Oh yeah?

ISAAC   She was like that girl from our neighbourhood, do you remember the Patel girl?

SAHIV   There were five hundred Patel girls, yaar!

ISAAC   No, *that* Patel girl, with the…

SAHIV   Oh! Yah, I remember her...

MR. X   What are we doing? Talking about our fares, like
               they were people.

ISAAC   They are people...

MR. X   Oh yes? Is that how you think they see us? I took this
               guy, this uptown guy, to the steam bath the other
               night. Y'know, where the gays meet for sex? I'm
               driving him, and I see in the back mirror—he rolls
               up a sleeve because the heat is too high—and I see
               his arm. He had a lesion. It was small, but he had
               it. He had signs of fatigue, and another small lesion
               just on the inside of the nasal passage. It was AIDS,
               man, it was textbook. I tell him, "I am a pathologist,
               you need treatment," and he laughs at me. He *laughs*
               at me. "Dr. Taxi Cab, you just lost your tip." And he
               gets out. And he goes to spread disease. *(pause)* They
               don't believe in me, Isaac. I don't believe in them,
               either. I hope he dies.

ISAAC   There is no cure to this. We cannot fix this. X used
               to say that we would find a way. He doesn't say that
               anymore. These broken promises... they take their
               toll on all of us. They make us lesser men. And for

a moment, that afternoon… for a moment I was worse than even that.

That afternoon. Yes. *(beat)* Things change so quickly…

He trails off for a moment, then continues.

Pinhead's father took ill, suddenly. He flew back to India but was too late. That afternoon he was returning home, and we were to meet him at the airport.

X and Sahiv in the limo, Sammy and I in my newly paid-off taxi. I drive, Sammy makes signs that read: "Dr. Pinhead M.D." to hold up at arrivals.

We're driving along the DVP, just at the Gardiner on-ramp, when BANG. A truck loses control in front of me. We are passing above the Don River, and there is no shoulder. Only two lanes, winding upwards, sixty feet off the ground.

The truck begins to jackknife, and we quickly edge around and in front of it. One more car behind me tries to get around… a white BMW. The truck crushes it before smashing through the guardrail and hanging off the bridge.

Suddenly, my cab is surrounded by people, like rush hour on Bay Street.

PEOPLE   What happened? Oh my God! Jesus, is he alive?

ISAAC   It's okay! I'm okay!

PEOPLE   Not you, asshole. They rush past me, towards my trunk. My trunk, on my newly waxed, newly paid-off taxi… where a motionless man lies stained in blood. The driver of the white BMW.

ISAAC   Please, give him room! *(pause, no reaction)* Don't try to move him! *(Pause, he grows more frustrated.)* Stop! Please! *(pause, then yells)* I'm a doctor!

CPR DUMMY   Whatever you say, Apu. I'm a certified lifeguard, I know what I'm doing.

ISAAC   They are about to roll him off my trunk. I am about to watch a man die because these people don't *believe* I'm a doctor. And right then, I want them to. I want them to kill this man. To kill him so they will learn that they are wrong and I am right. *(pause)* "I'm a fucking doctor, you fucking assholes!"

MR. X   Don't listen to him! He's a terrorist! He blew up
             the truck! Run! Run!

ISAAC   I have never seen people move so fast.

MR. X   Run! He's going to blow up the bridge! Call the
             police!!!

ISAAC   X! Stop that, man!

They approach ISAAC's trunk.

             Sahiv, check the truck driver, see if he's alive. Sammy,
             find my bag in the back seat. X, help me check this
             fucker's pulse. Fucking wax job, it's shit now…

             The man on my trunk has a faint pulse, but his eyes
             are rolled up like sushi and his skin has gone clammy.

             He's in shock.

MR. X   We should go. The police and ambulance will be
             here soon…

ISAAC   No they won't. *(pause, then sternly)* They *won't*. Traffic
             is fucked, they can't get around the truck chassis,

61

and the only other way on here is to go all the way around the river. He'll be dead by then.

They all stand around me. Their feet shuffle…

X spins his car keys around his index finger, like a gunslinger.

MR. X   What are you going to do, Isaac? You drive taxis.

ISAAC   I am a doctor.

MR. X   Not to him.

I look down at this man, lying on my cab. I think about the way those people looked at me when I told them I was a doctor. I think about my piece of paper sitting in my doctor's bag, wrinkling and yellowing and turning to dust. And right then, I agree with X. And I twirl my car keys like a gunslinger. Until Sammy pulls the man's wallet out of his coat and opens it. An ID tag from Toronto Western Hospital falls out.

ISAAC   He's a doctor. This man is a doctor.

MR. X grabs the card and studies it.

MR. X   That makes one of us.

ISAAC   X. What are we doing? Are we leaving this man?

MR. X   Leave him, we can't help.

ISAAC   No, you are a doctor, not a taxi-wallah!

MR. X   *I am neither!*

Long pause.

ISAAC   We are silent for days. Death gets closer to the man
               on my trunk. After a while, I reach into my doctor's
               bag, and I pull out my paper, on which is written
               the oath we all took.

               And I wasn't trying to make a point. I just… wanted
               to read it.

               I will neither prescribe nor administer a lethal dose
               of medicine to any patient even if asked nor counsel
               any such thing nor perform act or omission with
               direct intent deliberately to end a human life.

Pause.

63

X? We are dogs to these people. *(beat)* But, X…
To this man… To *this* man: You are a *cure*. *(beat)*
Gentlemen. Let's go to work.

We glove up as the man on my trunk stops breathing.

SAHIV   He's choking!

ISAAC   We need to secure an airway. I have a box cutter
and some pens in my bag, Sammy. Prep them for
me. *(He does.)* Okay, this is going to happen very
quickly. A cricothyroidotomy is an incision in the
thyroid above—

SAHIV   Yes, Isaac, we went to medical school as well.

Beat. ISAAC shrugs.

ISAAC   Okay. Eleven blade. *(pause)* What the hell is this?
Why do you give me scissors?

SAMMY   You asked for a blade!

ISAAC   An *eleven* blade, Sammy! Does this look like an eleven blade? Give me the box cutter!

SAMMY   Well if you wanted the box cutter, just say "Sammy, give me—"

ISAAC   Give me the fucking box cutter!

Forty-five seconds later, he is breathing again. But his pulse is still getting weaker. He needs blood.

Sammy, check the BMW, I need syringes, he might have some.

He does.

His donor card says his blood is B negative.

There is only one of us with that exact blood type.

X… you're a match.

Pause.

I wonder if I will have to read the oath again, but it will be rather anticlimactic.

X. Please.

X hangs his head, and his shoulders fall to the ground. He's crying. Weeping like a boy.

MR. X   This is what it takes to practice medicine in this country?

ISAAC   I don't know what to do. So I start to laugh. We all do. X turns around, tears streaming down his smiling face. He rolls up his sleeve.

MR. X   Doctor…

ISAAC   We break open the syringes and begin a positive flow into the white doctor's arm. After a few minutes, his face begins to colour and his pressure rises. We did it. We saved a man's life. We begin singing. Dancing, too.

The police arrive, we are forced to the ground at gunpoint, still singing. Our cars are impounded and we are held without bail. But the white doctor—whose name was Brown, ironically—he did not press charges.

And you must understand this, now. He was grateful. Very grateful. When we were released he shook our hands, one by one. He, too, cried. He praised our work. He praised our ethics. He praised a lot of things.

It meant nothing. *(pause)* Here's what did:

As we are leaving the impound lot, X pulls up with Pinhead (who forgave us for missing his flight).

MR. X   Wait! I stopped by your houses before I came. The only one I couldn't find was Isaac's.

Our diplomas. He is shoving our medical school diplomas through our windows. I take mine out of the special pocket in my doctor's bag. Ceremoniously, we replace our licence numbers, our hack papers... with our real credentials. We drive out the way we arrived... as doctors.

This city... this country... may not know who we are. But that day... we knew. And maybe we'll never get to practice medicine again, not the way we used to—and certainly not the way we did on that bridge, that afternoon. But we find a way. We find a way.

The ride is over. The passenger pays, gets out. ISAAC *smiles. He drives on.*

acknowledgements

Thanks to Nina Lee Aquino, Yvette Nolan, Sasa Jeric, Keira Loughran, Anita Majumdar, Isaac Thomas, Marion Brooks, Mickey Ko, Camie Koo, Matt White, Kory Bertrand and everyone involved in the many (many) iterations of these plays.

David Yee was born and raised in Toronto, and proudly identifies himself as a Hapa of Scottish and Chinese descent. A Dora Mavor Moore Award–nominated actor and playwright, his work has been produced across Canada and internationally. His play *lady in the red dress* was nominated for the 2010 Governor General's Literary Award. He is currently the artistic director of fu-GEN Asian Canadian Theatre Company.